PRE-CLOSING

FOR NETWORK MARKETING

"Yes" Decisions
Before The Presentation

Keith & Tom Big Al Schreiter

Pre-Closing For Network Marketing
© 2017 by Keith & Tom "Big Al" Schreiter

Published by Fortune Network Publishing
PO Box 890084
Houston, TX 77289 USA

Telephone: +1 (281) 280-9800

Second Edition
ISBN-13: 978-1-948197-00-7
ISBN-10: 1-948197-00-6

CONTENTS

PREFACE

It should be so obvious, but it isn't.

I had lunch with a lady in Romania. She complained, "Nobody in my small city wants to join. They all say it is a pyramid, they don't want to be a salesman, it is too good to be true, and they don't have time. What should I do?"

I asked, "So what did you tell them when you first met them?"

She said, "I have a wonderful business opportunity. You can earn $25,000 a month!"

I asked, "Is this what you told everyone? Is this how you started the conversation?"

She said, "Yes. Every time I talk to prospects, that is how I start the conversation."

I couldn't resist. I had to smile and tell her, "So, let me review. You say to every prospect, 'I have a wonderful business opportunity. You can earn $25,000 a month.' And your prospects tell you they are not interested, right? So why don't you say ... something different?"

Yes, that should be obvious.

Our prospects react to what we say and what we do.

Don't like their reactions? All we need to do is say something different.

For example, the lady in Romania could change her first few words to say things like:

- "Things sure are expensive now."
- "Sure would be fun to fire the boss."
- "We all need extra money."
- "We don't want to work hard for the rest of our lives."
- "Working from home would be easier than traveling to work."

Do you think her prospects would react more positively to those opening statements? Of course.

Changing the first words in our conversation will get a different reaction from our prospects.

So, if our prospects are negative, we can fix this by changing what we say and what we do.

Ah, but here is the problem. We don't know what to say differently.

And that is the reason for this book.

I travel the world 240+ days each year.
Let me know if you want me to stop in your
area and conduct a live Big Al training.

→ **BigAlSeminars.com** ←

FREE Big Al Training Audios
Magic Words for Prospecting
plus Free eBook and the Big Al Report!

→ **BigAlBooks.com/free** ←

PRE-CLOSING?

Think of pre-closing as a few phrases or sentences that we say early in our conversations with prospects. This all happens before we start our official presentation. These words prepare our prospects to think, "Yes, I want this!"

With pre-closing, the end of our presentation feels more normal. No high-pressure close is needed. No more begging. No more pushing. Pre-closing makes the end of our presentations easier for us and for our prospects.

Why pre-close?

Because our prospects make up their minds quickly. One of the first decisions our prospects will make is:

"Should I believe what you say? Or should I resist and disbelieve everything you say?"

This happens right away.

Here is reality. We say to our prospects, "Come with me to this business opportunity meeting." Our prospects think back to the last time they heard that phrase. They think, "Oh no! I went to my friend's house and someone gave a three-hour business opportunity presentation. Then, they high-pressured me to buy some overpriced stuff I didn't want."

Our prospects make a "no" decision, based upon past experiences.

Pre-closing? A good idea. Because we want open-minded prospects who will listen to what we're offering. We want them to make a decision to turn off their salesman alarms and listen.

Network marketing leader Wes Linden says, "Our job isn't to close people, it is to open them."

And the sale might not be immediate. Patricia Fripp says it another way. "To build a long-term, successful enterprise, when you don't close a sale, open a relationship."

Our prospects will make decisions before, during and after our presentation.

Closing doesn't just happen one time at the end of our presentations. As we will soon see, most decisions happen before our presentations begin!

Focus on this: "Pre-closing. Get 'yes' decisions before the presentation. Get agreements throughout the presentation. Get commitment to buy or join at the end of the presentation."

Closing is what we do as salespeople. Our job is to get our prospects to make decisions.

So let's look at some ways to get our prospects to:

1. Make instant "yes" decisions.

2. Decide to listen with an open mind.

3. Believe the good things we say.

4. Turn off their salesman alarms, and more.

Want a little preview? Some examples of fun opening questions that help pre-close prospects?

To keep things simple, all of these examples are for our business opportunity. Each example can be modified for the products and services we sell.

"Would it be okay if I share a little more about our business, while giving you a few ideas of where you can spend the extra money?"

This little question gets people to imagine where they could spend their extra money. This puts prospects in a positive frame of mind while we explain our business. Think about it. Would we want our prospects to be in a positive frame of mind or a negative frame of mind when we present our business? A positive one, of course.

Another factor enters this conversation. In order to imagine where to spend the money, the prospect's subconscious mind makes a decision to join the business. If not, this dreaming wouldn't make much sense. So for the moment, our prospect is immediately in the frame of mind that this business would be good for him.

"Would you like to know how I put away a bunch of money?"

Everyone would like to know this. We can describe how we took our monthly bonus checks and saved or invested them over time. Our explanation might take just a few sentences. But again, our prospects feel good about their possibilities. They see hope.

"Staying here at our job until we die, and not changing anything, is a plan. But I don't feel that it is a good plan for me. What about you?"

This question is a bit more aggressive, but may be appropriate with prospects we have a good relationship with. Our prospects might be in a rut. This question could shock our prospects into looking at their life plans.

There is nothing to disagree with in this statement. We only mention that staying at the job is "a" plan. Not the only plan. Anyone could agree with that statement.

"Why do you think extra income would be a good idea?"

When our prospects answer this question, they sell themselves on wanting an extra check. And who is a better salesman for our prospects? They are. They can sell themselves that this is their idea. They will convince themselves to say "yes" to an extra paycheck.

"So, do you think keeping your current plan, working at your job, is going to be the answer?"

Of course the current plan isn't working. If our prospects' current plan worked, they wouldn't be talking to us. The prospects respond, "Yes, the current plan isn't working." Now they open their minds, and look for a new solution. We should be that solution.

"Who do you think cares how much is in our savings account ten years from now?"

Say this, and then wait. Don't break the silence. Allow our prospects to mentally see how few people care about their situation. This helps our prospects overcome the "I wonder what other people will think about me?" objection that nags them from the back of their minds.

"How long will you receive a salary after you leave your job? Will your company still benefit from your work after you leave?"

Residual income is hard for prospects to grasp. Yes, it sounds good, but it doesn't seem real. Our prospects think, "When I stop working, my salary stops immediately!"

Now we can help our prospects see things from a whole new perspective. We want them to think, "Yes, I would like to do good work now, and get paid over and over again." This is a great mindset for our prospects when we start our presentation.

These little opening statements are fun. Pre-closing is powerful. But pre-closing solves other problems too. Let's look at one of these problems.

Tell our prospects that it is okay to say "no" to our offer.

Maybe our team members are having trouble with prospects saying, "I want to think it over." But when is the best time to prevent this from happening? At the start of our presentation. We can teach our team to do a pre-closing statement before they explain their product, service or opportunity. For example, they could say,

"I will show you our business, but it is entirely up to you. After I show you our business, you can decide not to participate, and keep things in your life as they are. Or, you can decide to start now, and begin the countdown to firing your boss. Sound okay?"

What would our prospects naturally say to this offer? "Okay."

This relaxes prospects, but also tells our prospects that they have to make a decision when we finish. And, the "I need to think it over" decision is a "no" decision. Now prospects know that.

This gets even better. Because of our opening statement, our prospects don't feel pressured. We gave our prospects permission to reject our presentation or offer. The prospects can now focus on our presentation and how it can help them.

What if we don't relax our prospects with this kind of language?

Then our prospects will look for objections. Why? Because our prospects feel that they will need objections to justify a "no" decision. Our prospects will be preparing themselves for a battle with us at the end of our presentation.

Want another simple way of removing the "I need to think it over" objection?

Prospects hate making decisions. They are afraid of making a wrong decision. So what do they do?

They pretend to delay the decision by saying that they need to think it over.

All we have to do is tell prospects:

"You can make a decision to start today, or you can make a decision not to start today and keep your life exactly like it is right now."

This helps prospects realize that there is always a decision made. Delaying a decision is just another way of saying "no" to the offer.

We can enhance the effect of this even more by reminding our prospects of their problems. For example, we could add:

"Suffering day after day at a job we hate is bad, especially if we make a decision to continue doing this for months or years before we do anything about it."

Pre-closing makes closing easy.

There are many ways to pre-close prospects. There will be at least one way that we will love. We don't have to use all of the pre-closing techniques we will learn in this book, but we will have to use some.

Why? Because they work.

Let's build our network marketing business faster by using pre-closing skills when talking to prospects.

"LET'S SORT IT OUT."

Let's learn another quick pre-closing technique now.

Are you a little bit shy? Or do you hate being pushy?

Try this easy phrase: "Let's sort it out now."

Let's say that you sold utility services. Here is an example of a conversation that pre-closes prospects, before the presentation begins.

Distributor: "Do you get an electricity bill?"

Prospect: "Yes."

Distributor: "Would you like them to send you a lower bill?"

Prospect: "Sure."

Distributor: "Okay. Let's sit down and sort this out now."

Done.

This conversation got to the point ... immediately.

Most people are happy to make a quick "yes" or "no" decision. They want to invest their limited and precious brainpower into other tasks. They want us to get to the point so they can make an immediate decision.

Want some more examples?

Distributor: "Do you want to lose an extra 10 pounds in the next few weeks?"

Prospect: "Yes."

Distributor: "Would it be okay if all you had to do is change what you have for breakfast?"

Prospect: "Sure."

Distributor: "Okay. Let's sit down and sort this out now."

◇◇◇◇

Distributor: "Do you want to stop commuting to that job you hate?"

Prospect: "Yes."

Distributor: "Would it be okay if we start your own business now, so next year you can work from home?"

Prospect: "Sure."

Distributor: "Okay. Let's sit down and sort this out now."

◇◇◇◇

Distributor: "Do you find it hard to get by on one paycheck?"

Prospect: "Yes."

Distributor: "Would it be okay if we start your own business now, so in 60 days you can have two paychecks instead of one?"

Prospect: "Sure."

Distributor: "Okay. Let's sit down and sort this out now."

◇◇◇◇

Distributor: "Do you want to keep that job you hate for the rest of your life?"

Prospect: "No."

Distributor: "Would it be okay if we got you started in a business tonight so you could start your training this weekend?"

Prospect: "Sure."

Distributor: "Okay. Let's sit down and sort this out now."

◇◇◇◇

Distributor: "Do you want to keep your skin from wrinkling while you sleep?"

Prospect: "Yes, of course."

Distributor: "Would it be okay if you tried our special night-time miracle cream for 30 days to see how much of a difference it would make?"

Prospect: "Sure."

Distributor: "Okay. Let's sit down and sort this out now."

◇◇◇◇

Distributor: "Do you find it hard to cover everything with just one paycheck?"

Prospect: "Yes, of course."

Distributor: "Would it be okay if we had lunch with a friend of mine, and we could see how you could get an extra paycheck also?"

Prospect: "Sure."

Distributor: "Okay. Let's sit down and sort out a time now."

◇◇◇◇

Distributor: "Do you want to be your own boss, instead of working someone else's hours?"

Prospect: "Yes."

Distributor: "Would it be okay if you joined me in a new part-time business I am starting? It would be fun to work together."

Prospect: "Sure."

Distributor: "Okay. Let's sit down and sort this out now."

Are all conversations this easy? No. But many are. Most prospects want to make a decision quickly and get on with their lives. Let's give them that option.

But what if they want to know more details? Great! That means they have already made a "yes" decision in their minds. If their answer was a "no" decision, they wouldn't be asking us to torture them with additional information.

Is "Let's sort this out" the only phrase we can use?

Certainly not. Let's try a few other examples using slightly different wording.

◇◇◇◇

Distributor: "Do you have electricity in your home?"

Prospect: "Yes, of course."

Distributor: "Would it be okay if they sent you a lower bill?"

Prospect: "That would be great."

Distributor: "Let me fix that for you now."

◇◇◇◇

Distributor: "Have you ever noticed that getting old really hurts?"

Prospect: "I notice that every day!"

Distributor: "Would it be okay if you could feel younger by drinking a shot of this every morning?"

Prospect: "If that is all it takes, sure."

Distributor: "Let me order you a few bottles now."

◇◇◇◇

Distributor: "Waiting in the freezing rain for the train to work is miserable."

Prospect: "I completely agree."

Distributor: "Should we make an escape plan for our jobs?"

Prospect: "I would love to, but I don't know where to start."

Distributor: "Let's have coffee with my sponsor on Saturday. He has some ideas."

◇◇◇◇

Pre-closing magic.

Ask any prospect, "Would you like a long presentation or a short presentation?"

The answer? "Please, give me the short presentation ... right now."

It only takes prospects a few sentences to decide if they want to join or not. It is the same with customers. They will know immediately if they want our offer or not.

We shorten our offer to just the basics and everyone is happy. When we simplify our offer, we simplify the decision for our prospects.

We are in the "closing business."

What is our job description as network marketers?

To get prospects to make a decision to buy our products and services, or to join our business. That is it.

We are not in the education business. Our companies don't pay us to educate people who don't buy or join.

We are not in the presentation business. We don't earn commissions on prospects who don't buy or join.

We don't get paid for making lists of prospects, calling for appointments, sending strangers to watch videos, having relatives listen to audios, sharing and caring, reading brochures to bored prospects as if they are reading-impaired, or passing out endless samples until we are bankrupt.

The only thing we get paid for is ... getting "yes" decisions from our prospects.

Until we embrace this reality, we will waste hours doing activities that don't lead to "yes" decisions.

Okay, that makes sense.

If we get people to make "yes" decisions, we get paid. That sums up our career.

But the real question in our minds should be, "How do prospects make their decisions?" The answer to this question might be the most fascinating discovery in our career.

Understanding the "how and when" of prospects' decisions is more important than reading sales training books for the rest of our career.

Let's get started.

#1. Why do people hate to sell?

Because they believe in the 1960s sales model of pushing products and services on other people.

The old model worked like this:

Make cold calls. Lots of cold calls. Pitch anyone and everyone who will listen. And if we get an appointment, dump on the prospect everything that we know about our product or service. Sell, sell, sell.

After we beat our glazed-eyed prospects into submission, then we go for the close. We use trial closes, hard closes, any close that could shame our prospects into buying. And if they don't buy immediately? Then we follow up. We harass our prospects until they buy or die!

Does that sound like fun? Of course not. Nobody wants to sell that way. Yet many people today are still using the old way of selling. This is not how prospects buy anyway. It is out of sync with the buying process.

Would we like to be sold this way? This is not how we buy, is it?

This explains call reluctance, fear of prospects, and why people don't want to join our business.

But there is a new way of selling. It's a way of selling that is in sync with how our prospects want to buy. Once we embrace it, everything gets easy.

So ask yourself, "Do I want to continue using the selling practices of the 1960s? Or would it be more fun if I talk to prospects so they want to buy?"

Here is the short story.

Prospects want to know the big picture first. They can immediately make a decision, based upon the stored programs in their minds. If the answer is "yes," then, and only then, should we begin a presentation.

Yes, in the first 20 seconds we know if we want something or not.

If this seems strange, it is because we are stuck in the mindset of the 1960s. Not good.

If this seems reasonable - that our prospects can make their final decision within the first 20 seconds - then we are in sync with our prospects. No more presentations until our prospect makes a "yes" decision.

Want some examples of this more humane, new way of selling?

◇◇◇◇

Distributor: "I help families get an extra paycheck. Would you like to know more?"

Prospect: "Yes. Tell me more." (Yes, I would like to have an extra paycheck. Give me some details to support my eager "yes" decision.)

◇◇◇◇

Distributor: "I show families how to get lower utility bills, so they have more money for other things. Would this be useful for you?"

Prospect: "Yes. Tell me more." (Yes, I am sold. Give me the details.)

◇◇◇◇

Distributor: "I market a breakfast protein drink that helps us lose weight one time, and keep it off forever. Is this something that sounds interesting?"

Prospect: "Yes. Tell me more." (I want to lose weight. I will try anything!)

◇◇◇◇

Distributor: "I help retail clerks start a new career, so they never have to work weekends again. Is this something that you would like to talk about?"

Prospect: "Yes. Tell me more." (I don't want this job for the rest of my life. Can we talk in the food court during my coffee break?)

◇◇◇◇

Wait a minute. This doesn't seem right!

Feels a little strange, doesn't it? Why would people mentally make an instant "yes" decision before they hear the details? This goes against our beliefs about how people make up their minds.

But it is "what we don't know" that holds us back. If we keep operating on what we know, then our results will stay the same. We want different results. So we will have to explore and find "what we don't know" to move our career forward.

Is there any shame in not knowing how to do a business before we start? Of course not. The only shame is to join a new profession, and then refuse to learn the new skills that the profession requires.

#2. Let's go to the movies.

Our good friend comes to our home and says, "Let's go to the movies. The new Disney movie opens today."

We drive to the movie theater. After standing in line for several minutes, we buy our overpriced tickets. Once inside, we see tasty snacks at "value pricing." So we invest in some popcorn with extra butter, a giant soda, and a few candy bars to hold us over during the movie.

We take our seats, and immediately the theater starts showing us commercials! Yes, we paid for our overpriced tickets and snacks, and now they are trying to sell us more with their commercials. After 15 minutes of commercials, we want to riot. But thankfully, now the trailers for the upcoming movies begin to show. The new movies look exciting. The mega-decibel speakers make our eardrums hurt. However, we enjoy the action on the screen.

Finally, the new Disney movie begins. For the next 90 minutes we are swept away in a fantasy world. We love movies.

When the movie finishes, the credits scroll down the screen. They tell us who produced the movie, who directed the movie, who did the lighting, who made the refreshments for the production crew, the locations in the filming, the names of all the major actors and minor actors, the year the movie was made, that Disney owns all rights, and way more information than we have any interest in.

Now, here is the question.

We have a timeline from when our friend came to our home all the way to the credits scrolling on the screen at the end of the movie. Let's think about this.

"At what point during this timeline, between our friend coming over and the movie finale, did we make our final decision to go to the movie?"

And the answer is … immediately!

We made our final decision to go to that movie before we bought our tickets, and before we saw the movie. All the details and information happened **after** we made the decision to go to that movie. In fact, most of the details and information about the movie happened **after** we saw the movie!

#3. Women hate this.

The husband relaxes to watch television. He grabs his favorite tool, the remote control. Then what happens?

Click. Click. Click … and more clicks. The husband mindlessly clicks through every channel looking for something he wants to watch.

How long does it take the husband to make a decision for each channel? Less than a few seconds.

The man makes his final decision with almost no facts, almost no information. The man doesn't watch the entire show. He decides in less than two seconds if that show is for him or not.

We think, "Hey, that's not fair. He needs to know more. He needs to watch the channel longer." Well, it may not be fair, but that's how it is.

The man has a mechanism inside of his brain that automatically makes the final decision about that channel, and this mechanism works in seconds. No facts needed.

Our prospects use this same mechanism to make their final decision about our business. They don't make their decision based on facts or information. So please, let's not irritate our prospects with facts and information when we are seeking a decision. That would be rude.

Let's save our video and presentation book for later, after the decision. They will make excellent training tools if our prospects decide to join or buy.

Wow!

So let's ask ourselves this question, "When do people make their final decision? After the information happens, or before?"

It appears ... before the information!

Ouch. This changes our beliefs about decisions.

Our observation shows us that information is not part of our prospects' decision-making criteria. The information happens after our prospects' final decision. And the "yes" or "no" decision happens ... instantly???

A new view.

We should be feeling a little bit uncomfortable at this moment. This is not how we thought prospects made decisions.

Instant decisions based on no information means … oh my! My wonderfully-crafted presentation may not be as important as I thought it was. In fact, it may be meaningless in our pursuit of getting a decision from our prospects.

Hard to believe?

We can doubt brain science. We can be skeptical about all the psychological research. But it is difficult to dismiss our honest observation of the facts. People make decisions instantly, based upon little or no information.

#4. Let's go grocery shopping.

It is time for our weekly trip to the grocery store. As we grab the cart, we head down the first aisle. Immediately to our left, we see a carton of milk. Would we think this?

"All right! Milk! I hope the milk company has a video explaining the history of cows. Maybe the video can show me pictures of their farm and the cows they milk. I wonder if the company founder always loved the cow business. Is there some online audio where I can hear the milking machines in action? I need to check the back of the milk carton to see if they have a list of the awards they won in milk-grading contests. There doesn't seem to be a PowerPoint presentation, but maybe there are audio testimonials of people who drink their milk. If their milk was patented, that would be impressive."

If those are the thoughts that cross our mind, we have a problem. People don't think this way. We simply look at the carton of milk and make an instant decision to buy it or not.

Then, we continue walking and looking at more grocery items. As we walk, our mind continues making these instant decisions. "No, no, no, yes to those candy bars, no, no, yes to those snacks, no, no, no."

Is there any thinking involved? No. All of these instant decisions were made by stored programs in our minds.

If we did not make decisions this way, and needed an hour-long presentation about each item in the aisle, we would starve before we got to the end of the grocery store aisle. Thankfully, our minds don't work like that.

We can't deny the obvious.

Our prospects make instant and immediate decisions based upon little or no information.

The decisions to buy or join happen early in the conversation. These decisions do not happen after a 45-minute, mind-numbing presentation.

If information was enough, then network marketing companies would not need us. The Internet is full of information. Add to that brochures and catalogs by the millions.

But ... don't prospects need information?

Information is the weight that holds us back and slows our career growth. Prospects don't need information. Information is not what prospects use to make decisions. Want proof?

Let's talk about overweight people. I am one of them. As an overweight person, I have brochures, research reports, audios, videos, and documentaries on how to lose weight. I live next to weight-loss clinics, gyms, and diet consultants. Every day I see dieting information on television and on the Internet. I have been preached to and lectured to on how to lose weight. Every overweight person in the universe, including me, has the information on how to lose weight.

Ask any overweight person, "How do you lose weight?" What will they say? "Eat less food, and exercise more." Every overweight person in the universe got the information!

So here is the question.

If people made decisions on information, and every overweight person in the universe has the information, wouldn't that mean that there would be no overweight people?

Ouch!

All that information has nothing to do with the decisions people make. So every time we see an overweight person over the next two weeks, simply say to ourselves (inside our minds, please, not out loud), "People don't make decisions based on information."

There we have it. Every time we see someone who is overweight, it proves to us that information has nothing to do with decisions.

Will everyone on your team accept that decisions work this way?

No. Amateur distributors won't believe their presentations have nothing to do with their prospect's decision. They will argue:

- "But they have to know the name of the company."
- "They need to know about our patented products."
- "How can they decide without first seeing our compensation plan?"
- "We are the best. They have to know that first."
- "Our scientist can beat up other companies' scientists."
- "Nobody decides until they see the facts."
- "Our wonderful company video is what sells prospects."
- "My 3-D laminated flip chart presentation is what causes them to decide."

It is hard to argue with amateur distributors. They don't know what they don't know - yet.

So what would we do?

Tell them, "Figure it out."

Give them these two examples. They either "get it," or they doom themselves to long, boring, useless presentations. Here are the examples.

Example #1. We invite a prospect to our opportunity meeting. He doesn't come. Has he made his decision? Yes. What was his decision? "No." He decided not to join and he hasn't seen a single fact or bit of information.

Example #2. We invite a prospect to our opportunity meeting. He decides not to have dinner with his family. He decides not to watch television that evening. He decides not to rest after a hard day's work. Instead, he decides to give up his entire evening so that he can come to our meeting and start his own business.

And he hopes we don't talk him out of it with a long, boring presentation. When did he make his decision? Before he came to our meeting.

Yes, prospects make the final decision before the facts.

This goes against all our amateur distributors' beliefs. They will resist adjusting their business to take advantage of this fact. People hate to change their beliefs.

Our amateur distributors will continue to force presentations on prospects who make "no" decisions. This is impolite, and wastes the time of everyone involved.

The result? Frustration for both the prospect and the amateur distributor.

Pre-closing? Now, that makes sense.

Prospects make their final decision based on no information, and before our presentation begins. So how we use the time before the presentation can determine whether we get that final "yes" decision.

Pre-closing works in our favor. Why? Because it is comfortable for our prospects. High-pressure closing techniques at the end of the presentation just don't make sense.

The reality of our first contact.

Our prospects have many decisions to make every second.

- Should I stand or sit?
- Do I pay attention to that car across the street?
- Will I get home in time to watch my favorite shows?
- Am I hungry? Let me check.
- Do I have time to think about my spouse's birthday present now?
- Was my boss honest in my job review?

When we meet prospects, they want to make a decision about us and our offer as quickly as possible. They have too many other decisions fighting for their attention. That is why they rush their initial mental "yes" or "no" decision.

This is how we think. This is how our prospects think. So why not use words and phrases that will make it easy for our prospects to make a quick decision? Less stress, less rejection, happier prospects.

CAN YOU RECRUIT 100 PEOPLE IN ONE WEEK?

Belief is important, but it is only the first step.

We get a telephone call. The person says, "Are you an investment banker? Can you raise money? Could you get $500,000 together that I can borrow next Thursday?"

Our answer? "I can't do that. I am not trained in raising capital. I don't even have friends that have extra money."

Because we don't believe that it is possible, we won't even try.

Belief is the first step. If we don't believe, all the skills in the world will not help us.

Now imagine this scenario.

We get a telephone call. The person says, "I kidnapped your child. I will release your child on Thursday for $500,000."

What do we say? We wouldn't say, "Oh, I am not a professional that can raise money. Sorry."

We say, "I will have $500,000 by Thursday."

What was the difference? Did we get new training? No. The difference was belief.

Without belief, we won't try. Even though we don't know how to raise $500,000 now, we believe that we could learn new skills and figure out a way before Thursday.

The first step is … belief.

Believing that we can is only the first step.

It is a necessary step, but there is another. The second step is learning what to say to our prospects.

For all the people who believe that just thinking positively about something will make it happen, I share this story.

The "We need skills" story.

The prospect says, "No."

And our reply?

We say, "No? Are you kidding? But I chanted affirmations this morning! And I have new pictures on my vision board. Yesterday I worked on my mindset. My goals are better than your goals. I attended two company conventions and yelled with enthusiasm. I jumped higher than everyone else. I believe so hard. I am passionate! So how can you refuse my offer???"

Okay, that's a ridiculous reply.

But it does point out that getting our heads right is only the first step towards success. Yes, it is a very important first step. But we have to do more.

Step #2: Learn the skills of our profession.

Unless we learn the skills of how to get our prospects to make "yes" decisions, we don't have a business. We have hope. We have wishes. But not a solid business. Our financial security and success depends on learning the skills of our profession. So let's ask ourselves, "When would be a good time to start learning these skills?"

Hopefully ... now!

We must master pre-closing so our prospects will make "yes" decisions instead of "no" decisions.

Let's learn a few more easy techniques now.

THE "BUILD VALUE" PRE-CLOSE.

Why do prospects complain about the cost of becoming a distributor? Because they don't see the value of our business. We can solve this problem by building value in our offer.

We can say something like this:

"So how much would it be worth to you to add an extra $500 a month to your regular income?"

Wait for an answer. Our prospects are thinking that our business is worth much more than $500.

We pause and wait. Our prospect now has to come up with an answer. And their answer will be many times more than $500.

Remember, the key is to allow our prospects the time to think about the value. Don't interrupt. The longer we wait, the more value is being added in our prospects' minds.

TALKING TO COLD LEADS? TWO AWESOME SENTENCES THAT MAKE IT EASY.

Calling cold leads is very difficult. There is no relationship. The prospects are skeptical. My friend, Jackie Clayton, solves this problem with two incredible questions.

When the prospects answer the phone, she says:

"I understand you have been looking for a home-based business. So tell me, why haven't you found a home-based business yet?"

What happens?

The prospects relax and tell Jackie why they are still looking. They explain what they liked and disliked about their research so far. They even tell Jackie what is holding them back.

The prospects do all the talking and feel comfortable in their conversation with Jackie.

Now Jackie knows exactly what they are looking for, and describes her business in a way that is acceptable to them.

This is better than mind-reading. When prospects tell us exactly what they like and don't like before we start a presentation, well, it doesn't get any easier than this.

Want another two-sentence opening?

We can prepare our prospects early in our conversation by saying:

"There are two types of people in the world. Those who look for reasons why, and those who look for reasons why not."

This puts our prospects in an open-minded attitude. They will naturally look for reasons why our opportunity can work for them instead of looking for reasons not to join.

When we use this phrase to start a presentation, we will notice that we don't have to use any high-pressure closing techniques. Prospects can fairly judge for themselves if this opportunity will fit their needs or not.

WANT TO SORT PROSPECTS IMMEDIATELY?

After listening and discovering our prospects' problems, we can say, "Do you want to do something about it?"

Our prospects have two possible answers.

Answer #1: "Yes."

That is easy. Now we can give a quick presentation, and we know our prospects will join or buy our product or service.

This is pre-closing at its easiest!

Prospects have problems. They want to fix their problems. Decision: "Yes!" And then we can leisurely explain some details in our presentation.

Answer #2: "No."

When our prospects don't want to fix their problems, we stop. We are talking to prospects to help them, not to make them unhappy. Some people are happier keeping their problems. They define themselves by their problems. For example, listen to these two sentences:

#1. "I am a diabetic." (This is part of me. This defines who I am as a person.)

#2. "I am a person with diabetes." (Diabetes is not who I am.)

Now, prospects can say "no" in hundreds of ways. Most of these ways sound like excuses. For example:

- "I want to think it over."
- "Is there a website I can go see?"
- "I will get back to you next week."

We could list more of these excuses, but we are already familiar with them. We hear them all the time.

And what should we do when our prospects make a "no" decision? Be polite. Respect their wishes. The reason our prospects want to tell us "no" is because they mean it. They are not interested.

But what if we know they really need it? Should we try to harass them and high-pressure them into a "yes" decision? No. Accept the fact that we didn't do a good enough job. It is time to go home and work on our rapport skills or some other step that we missed.

Our business can be stress-free, if we use this secret.

If some prospects are not interested, we should move on for now.

The purpose of business is to solve problems for our prospects. If some prospects don't have problems, or don't want to fix their problems, we respect their choices.

There are plenty of prospects who have problems that our products, services and opportunity could fix. We want to spend most of our time with these prospects. We don't want to spend that time with non-prospects.

MORE WAYS TO GET QUICK DECISIONS.

Ever have problems breaking the ice or getting prospects interested in hearing our presentation? Then start with small steps. Start with this question that begs for a "Yes."

"If I helped you start a part-time business, and then you got to retire two years later, would you send me a thank-you card?"

How could our prospect refuse?

The prospect is now leaning forward, in a positive frame of mind, and we can give a presentation rejection-free. That was easy. And it happened in seconds.

Let's try another one.

Fear of loss.

Many years ago, I heard a speaker end his presentation with a great close. But why use this close at the end of the presentation? Instead, we could use it before we start.

Why?

This close tells prospects how much our opportunity costs. Takes the pressure off of them. Plus, it makes us look confident that we are not concerned about the price of our business.

In addition, this close creates a "fear of loss" feeling in prospects. The fear of loss is always greater than the desire for gain. After hearing this close, prospects make a quick mental decision to open up their minds and look for reasons to join, instead of looking for reasons not to join.

Here is the closing statement:

"Folks, it takes $99 to say 'Yes' to our opportunity, and $2.5 million to say 'No.'"

In other words, for $99 you can get into our network marketing opportunity. That is cheap. However, if you say "No" and don't take advantage of our network marketing opportunity, you could lose out on $2.5 million in future bonus checks. You can't afford to decline this opportunity.

This powerful statement gets people to try our opportunity. And as an added bonus, prospects respect us for being up-front and telling them the full offer and price. They don't have to wait until the end to hear it.

A word of caution.

Powerful closing statements summarize our opportunity's benefits and get people to join. However, there is a difference between a decision of commitment and a decision of convenience.

Prospects who need the extra push to make a decision often are making a decision of convenience. It's easier for them to say "Yes" than it is to say "No" to us.

Decisions of convenience are weaker. That means we will have to build their commitment after joining. Why? Because they will need to be strong to overcome rejection, criticism and the many challenges we face while building a business.

Compare this type of "decision of convenience" prospect to a prospect who makes a "decision of commitment." When prospects are committed, they don't need artificial or powerful closing statements. They sell themselves before we start our presentation.

THE CURSE OF THE INFORMATION COLLECTORS.

When we talk to prospects, the only decision our prospects have to make is if they want to start a business ... or not. Or if they want to buy our products and services ... or not.

Why such a simple decision? Because our prospects can't make a fair decision on anything else. Think about it. At this point in the conversation, do our prospects have enough information:

- To evaluate a brand-new industry?

- To know the inside tricks and strategies to growth?

- To understand our compensation plan filled with industry jargon?

- To judge our products on their first glance or exposure?

- To even know what kind of questions to ask?

- To know how to do the job, even though they've never been in this business?

No! It is unfair to ask prospects to make a decision on all these issues outside of their expertise. They will learn these things after they decide to join our business, begin training, and get experience.

Just think back to how little we knew in our first week in our businesses.

What decision can our prospects make before we start our presentation?

They can decide if they want to do business with us ... or not. That is it.

But don't they have to know how to do our business before they start? No! That would be ridiculous. Don't allow the old excuse, "I can't join. I don't know how to do this."

To this excuse, say, "Of course you don't know how to do this business. The company doesn't expect you to know how to build a business before you join. That would be insane. That is why the company provides training after you join, so you can learn how to build your business effectively."

No one expects us to know how to build a network marketing business before we start.

Knowing how to build our new business comes later.

For now, the only decision that counts is if our prospects want to join our business or not.

1. If they want to join our business, now is a great time for them to enroll and start their training.

2. If they don't want to join our business now, this is a great time to know. We can stop harassing them and

let them get on with their lives. Maybe they will be ready in the future.

Once we know that getting the "join now" decision is our goal, it gets easy.

We can close on this decision early in our conversation. If we don't, here is the problem.

We talk, we mail samples, and we send these prospects to our webpages. Finally they have all the information about our opportunity and it is time for them to make a decision.

A decision to join? A decision to take action? A decision to go to work?

Panic time. So what does your "information-collecting" prospect do? He suddenly decides that he needs to investigate and research yet another opportunity.

And this is the life cycle of our "information-collecting" prospects. They spend their entire careers investigating, researching, and studying ... to avoid actually doing something.

They are experts at everything. They can tell you what is right or wrong about every opportunity and product. They publish their opinions and start discussion groups to regurgitate the same information over and over.

Eventually, these prospects do grow up and become ... critics.

This is the curse of the "information collectors."

Remember that long presentation with hours of questions? And then the prospect said he needed to think it over?

Frustrating, isn't it? Only then do we realize that some people don't want to start a business.

These "information-collecting" prospects feel like they are making progress investigating possibilities. The reality is they don't want to find something and then have to go to work.

Why? Because if they actually got started, they would have to work hard and risk rejection.

That is why they are forever researching. That wastes our time because we are dealing with non-prospects.

This excuse is common with analyzers such as engineers, accountants, data processing professionals, scientists, etc. Many would rather safely collect information instead of risking their first step into a business. They want to know endless details and think about their decisions forever. This drives us crazy.

Stop this tragedy and pre-close early. Simply say:

"Before I start, I want to make sure I talk about what you want. So are you looking to start a business now, and start earning money ... or are you in the information-collecting stage?"

This question stuns the analyzers and helps us focus on the big picture.

If they say they are looking to start a business now, we are done! Closed.

And if they are in the information-collecting stage, we give them some web links, a brochure, or something similar, and we can be on our way. They will be happy that we didn't try to get them started right away. We will be happy because we can spend our time with someone new, who wants to get started now.

When we have this big picture in mind, then it is easier for us to focus our conversation towards getting that one decision.

The first step is to get the commitment to start a business.

What if we don't get this commitment? Then we are talking to someone who isn't ready to join. That is a hard problem to fix. Our discussion goes nowhere.

But what if I already started my presentation?

If we are stuck in an endless loop of questions and details, we can say this to stop the time-sucking drama. This question puts us back on track to the big picture of whether now is the right time to join or not. We can say:

"Go ahead and collect all the information you want, but I would like to talk to you about the big picture. Would it be okay if we talked at a higher level?"

Most prospects will say, "Oh yes. Of course it is okay if we talk at a higher level."

And now we can redirect the conversation back to the prospect's decision: if they want to start a business now, or not.

Want another way to handle these information collectors?

Many questions are simply uneasiness about the prospect's future success. Rather than answer unending questions, consider this approach. Most of the more trivial questions could be answered with:

"We cover that in training. But the real question is, 'Do you want to join our business now, so that we can get you enrolled in training right away?'"

Still not enough options?

Then we can try this at the appropriate time in our conversation with our prospect.

"You are probably tired and bored with collecting more information and theory. So if you are ready to actually start building a business, when would be a good time to start? Or would you rather put off building a business for a few more months?"

This seems to sort out prospects pretty quickly.

Suppose your prospect says: "Oh, I need a few more weeks to think about how much money I would make if I actually knew how to build a business." Then we know it is time to leave our prospect alone.

We fulfilled our responsibility. We gave them the option of starting their business. We are not responsible for the final choices our prospects make.

And what if they keep asking for more details?

Well, we should be polite. If possible, we provide details, even though they have no way to evaluate them. But, we should ask ourselves this question: "Why are they asking for all these hard-to-evaluate details?"

The answer is, "Because they don't feel comfortable coming on our journey. They are afraid they will die on our journey. So now they are desperately grasping at details to give them some sense of security."

Security?

Yes.

Let's look at this from the prospect's point of view.

THE FIRST DECISION.

"It is what we don't know that kills us."

Another way of saying this is, "The definition of frustration is not knowing what we don't know. That means we can never know what we don't know, because we don't know what to learn."

Everyone in network marketing has felt this frustration at least once. Things go wrong, but we don't know why.

In my case, here is what happened. I gave hundreds of presentations, and no one joined. That is a problem. But I could not fix the problem, because I did not know the cause of the problem.

I tried guessing. I thought prospects needed more information. Of course, that wasn't true. Even though I doubled the amount of information and doubled the length of my presentation, no one joined.

But it got worse.

Several levels above me in my upline was a leader named Bob. Bob would sit down with a prospect and say, "Well ..."

And the prospect would immediately say, "I would like to join." What????

Yes. Bob would sit down for a few moments and prospects were begging to join him.

I hated Bob.

I worked hard every day, spent time away from my family, and I got no results. No matter how much I improved my presentation, nothing happened.

I had to watch Bob's success. Bob sat with prospects, smiled, said a word or two, and they joined! This was torture.

But Bob knew a secret.

Bob knew that people hate their lives. Wake up in the morning, go to work, go to sleep. Wake up in the morning, go to work, go to sleep. Wake up in the morning, go to work, go to sleep. Wake up in the morning, go to work ... die!

Yes, most people hate their lives. Bob knew this. People are desperately looking for a plan. They do not have a plan. If they had a plan, they would have followed it.

So imagine the typical prospects that I would have talked to.

1. They hated their lives.

2. They were looking for a plan. I had a plan.

3. They were looking for someone who knew where they were going. I knew where I was going.

4. And finally ... they wanted to know if that person had the skills to take them along safely. Oh my! This is where it all went wrong.

Prospects would look at me and think, "If I join you on your journey, I will die on the journey."

My prospects did not want to die. How did they know that they would die?

Prospects can smell desperation. Prospects can sense incompetency.

In just a few seconds, the programs in the back of their minds detected that if they joined me on my journey, they would die. They knew I didn't have the skills to take them along safely.

But I had a good attitude!

I thought positive thoughts! I sang the company song! I had new pictures on my vision board! And none of this mattered. The prospects were only concerned with getting to their destinations safely.

Humans think this way. Imagine that we get on an airplane. As we enter the airplane, the captain says, "Welcome aboard. I don't know how to fly this plane, but I have a pretty good attitude."

Are we getting on that airplane? No! Because we don't want to die.

And that is why they didn't join me on my journey, because they didn't want to die!

It is not a matter of attitude, it is also a matter of skills.

Prospects only want to come on our journey if they feel that they will arrive safely with us.

But back to Bob. Prospects sensed that Bob had the skills to get where he was going. They wanted to go there also. And they wanted to follow Bob on that journey.

That is the first test with prospects. I failed that test. Why? Because I thought their decision was about information, the industry, the company, the products, the compensation plan, and all the useless details. I didn't know that prospects made their decision before my presentation began.

So what is the bottom line?

Prospects make that decision quickly. The good news is that we only have to be competent for the first few seconds. If we can get the first 20 or 30 seconds correct, and do it with confidence, prospects will want to be on our team. They will make an immediate decision that they want to follow us on our successful journey.

How do we get this aura of competency? Two ways.

First, personal development. Nobody wants to follow a "gloom and doom" person. Personal development makes us better people. People want to be around better people. That is why we are attracted to positive people rather than negative people at parties.

Personal development gets us started.

But we need more. Nobody wants to follow a positive idiot on a suicide mission.

Second, we need hardcore skills. When we speak concisely, with the correct words, prospects "feel" our competency. They are confident that we know what we are doing, that we will get to our destination, and that they want to come with us.

Is pre-closing one of those skills that prospects look for? Of course. What we say early in our conversations will influence their decisions.

So what is the first test?

"If I go with you on your journey, will I arrive safely?"

Bob knew this. I did not.

Prospects make this decision long before we even mention the name of our company. We have to manage those critical first few seconds of our engagement with prospects. We want to be like Bob.

THE PURPOSE OF BUSINESS IS TO SOLVE OTHER PEOPLE'S PROBLEMS.

If no one got hungry, there would be no need for restaurants. If no one got sleepy, there would be no reasons for hotels to exist. And if people lived forever, selling vitamins would be difficult.

Network marketing is easy if we concentrate on solving other people's problems. But, how are we going to know what their problems are?

Not by talking. We have to listen.

If our new distributors come to us and ask, "What should I say?" … then they are missing the point. Instead of talking, they should worry about listening.

Listen?

Well, we don't want to mindlessly listen to the drama of our prospects' in-laws. That is why we will focus the conversation on our prospects' problems. Then, we can see if our products or opportunity can help solve their problems.

How do we focus the conversation on our prospects' problems? We ask the right questions.

Some questions to pre-close prospects.

Remember, the purpose of business is to solve problems.

Our job is to get our prospects to want to solve their problems now, not sometime in the vague future.

Problems are unpleasant. We don't want to think about our problems. So what do we do? We quickly move our thoughts elsewhere. We want to avoid the bad feelings that come with pondering the implications of our problems.

To motivate our prospects to solve their problems now, we get our prospects to spend more time thinking about their problems.

Problems become more urgent when our prospects think about them more. We create more urgency by asking more questions.

Here are some example questions that get prospects to think about and discuss their problems.

- When would be a good time to start your own business?

- How does it feel not having an extra paycheck every week?

- When would be a good time to earn extra checks for your family?

- How many pounds overweight should you be at age 50?

- How much should you be paying each month for your phone?

- To be paid fairly, how much should you earn per hour?

- How many weeks of vacation do you need each year?

- If you were your own boss, would you change anything?

- How big of a raise do you expect this year?

- Do you expect things will stay the same?

- Would you like luxurious eyelashes without pasting them on?

- How much per hour should lawyers charge?

- Wrinkles happen. At what age should they start?

- Do you know anyone who needs extra income?

- What about a five-day weekend?

Starting a conversation in the right direction is easy when we use great questions.

What should we ask first?

We ask questions to see if our prospects have problems. If they don't have problems, then there is nothing we can fix or help with.

Want to get better at asking questions?

Want to get our prospects to open up more, and tell us their most nagging problems?

Fortunately, people have lots of problems. Problems are easy to discover if we ask these two questions in the right order.

Question #1: "What do you like most about ..."

Question #2: "What do you like least about ..."

The answer to Question #1 is unimportant. We ask for the positives first to help our prospects relax. If we started digging deep immediately by asking for problems, our prospects would be hesitant and we would fall out of rapport.

The answer to Question #2 is what we want. This answer will tell us exactly how our product or business can solve problems for our prospects.

Here is an example.

Question #1: "What do you like most about your job?"

The prospect replies, "Well, the pay is okay. And it was my dream job out of school."

Question #2: "What do you like least about your job?"

The prospect replies, "I am stuck in an office all day. I never get out. Never get a chance to talk to people. I hate moving paper from one side of the desk to the other. I am a people-person."

And now we know exactly what to say to this prospect. Our presentation will focus on his problem, career dissatisfaction.

When we ask the proper questions, we locate the exact problems our prospects want to fix. Now our presentations are customized to them. Our presentation won't seem like some generic sales pitch.

A big part of the final decision made by prospects is, "Do you understand my situation?" By showing that we care, by asking the right questions, our prospects will want to do business with us.

Are these the only questions we could ask? Of course not. Let's do an example of some additional questions. We will imagine that we are selling diet products.

The five-question approach.

These five questions make it easy for our prospects to make an immediate decision, even before we begin our presentation. The best way to illustrate this is with an example. Ready?

Question #1: "If there was a way you could lose weight, have more energy, not be hungry, and never have to give up your favorite foods ... you would at least like to know about it, wouldn't you?"

Our prospects should say "yes" because we gave them four great benefits. They will like at least one of the benefits.

Question #2: "Have you ever dieted before?"

Listen to our prospects' answers. If they are grossly overweight, and have never dieted successfully before, we know we should focus on getting them to commit to a diet. Just talking about our special diet products would be wasting our breath.

Question #3: "What did you like **most** about your previous diets?"

Remember, this question is positive and non-invasive. We want our prospects to relax. We listen and make mental notes of any information that might be helpful later in our presentation. We ask this question so that we will have permission to ask the next question.

Question #4: "What did you like **least** about your previous diets?"

Our prospects will tell us what they didn't like about their previous diets. We can adjust our offering based upon what they liked and didn't like. For example, if they said they didn't like drinking protein shakes, we wouldn't include that product in their customized diet package. This question helps us to avoid offending our prospects by presenting something that they don't want.

Question #5: "What is the most important reason you want to lose weight?"

This answer will give us their motivation so we can handle their objections. Their emotional reasons will overcome price objections, time objections, etc. Common answers to this question might be:

- "I want to lose weight to look good in my daughter's wedding pictures. She gets married in three months and those pictures will be on the wall forever."

- "I want to lose weight to look good at my class reunion to spite my ex-girlfriends."

- "I want to lose weight because my doctor said I will die quickly if I don't."

- "I want to lose weight because my spouse will buy me a new wardrobe if I do."
- "When I play golf, my stomach is so big I can barely see the golf ball."

This is a nice little formula.

We can use these five questions as a template for our business opportunity, our products, and our services.

We ask these questions before our presentation. Let's see what we've accomplished.

Question #1: "If there were a way you could (insert some benefits) ... you would at least like to know about it, wouldn't you?"

We offer multiple benefits. Our prospects will like at least one of the benefits.

Question #2: "Have you ever (ask for previous experience) before?"

This will give us a clue about how our prospects make their decisions.

Question #3: "What did you like **most** about ...?"

This is an easy question for our prospects to answer. And because we ask this question, it will seem more natural for us to ask the next question.

Question #4: "What did you like **least** about ...?"

This is the most important question. The purpose of business is to solve problems. We have to find out our prospects' problems. This is the perfect question to accomplish that.

Question #5: "What is the most important reason you want to …?"

When we know our prospect's "why," it is easy to overcome objections. If their "why" is big enough, no objection will stand in their way. All we have to do is keep reminding our prospects of their "why."

Here is an example.

Our prospect tells us, "The most important reason I want to start a business? I hate waking up to the alarm clock every morning." Now, for almost any objection from this prospect we would say: "But you do want to get rid of that alarm, don't you?"

Imagine this prospect objected and said, "Oh, I don't know if I have enough time to start a part-time business." We would reply, "But you do want to get rid of that alarm, don't you?"

Prospects have problems. We can fix those problems. This is why prospects will love us.

MAKING PEOPLE THINK.

Most people go through life in a trance. They are in a rut, a routine, and go through the motions of daily life without thinking. And then, life slips by.

We can help. We can remind our prospects that they are in a trance. And we can at least offer one more option for their lives. The option? Network marketing, of course.

So how do we help prospects break free from their trances and take a good look at other options?

Simple conversation. And … questions.

When we ask our prospects a question, they have to stop and actually think.

What do we want our prospects to think? It would be great if they made a mental decision. "Hey! I want an opportunity to take me away from my day-to-day routine."

Here are some examples of questions that we could ask while we are having conversations with prospects.

- "I am thinking of escaping from the 9-to-5 rat race. What about you?"

No pressure. We simply ask if our prospects have ever had those thoughts. If our prospects agree with us, the rest of the conversation will be easy.

- "How many more days do you have before retirement?"

When our prospect starts counting, it seems like an eternity. And if our prospect hates his job, the feeling gets worse. We can even enhance those feelings by saying, "Well, you are only 4,879 days away from doing what you want to do."

Some novelty sites sell countdown clocks. We can buy a countdown clock and set it to the number of days our prospect has remaining in his job. If our prospect places this countdown clock on his desk, what will he think about every day while he struggles through his boring job?

- "Does your boss get paid a lot more, yet work fewer hours?"

When prospects are unhappy, they look for solutions. We can be their solution.

- "I wish I could quit my job and delete the alarm app from my phone. Have you ever had that feeling?"

No pressure. No rejection. Just conversation. But how easy will it be for prospects to agree with us? They will adopt our wishes as their own. Their current jobs don't offer them the chance to sleep late, but we can. If our prospects make a decision to change their lives and sleep late, we are the easy solution to their income needs.

- "I don't want next year to be like this year. I want something different. What about you?"

This is a great thing to say at a family reunion. Instead of skeptical relatives thinking we are pitching a business, now we have open-minded relatives who want more opportunity. If they make a decision for more opportunity in their lives, our continuing conversation will have total rapport.

- "I don't love this job. I do love the paycheck though. I am thinking about a more enjoyable way to get a paycheck. Ever have those thoughts?"

Sometimes we are in a rut so deep, we can't see out. People mentally "check out" and resign themselves to thinking, "I need money, so I have to keep this job."

Our job is to shock them out of their current trances, and help them take a look at more options.

- "You know how much we hate this job? I found an escape. I am taking it."

What is the first reaction from our co-worker? "Wait! Wait for me! I want to join your escape plan!"

- "I am going to have a new career next year. My new career will be having five coffee breaks a day, talking to interesting people."

What is our co-worker thinking? "I love coffee breaks. They are my favorite time of the day. And if I could have a career chatting with people over coffee, it would be awesome. So what do I have to do next to join your new career?"

- "We all know this job won't make us rich. So what is your plan to beat the system?"

Now our prospect has to think about his current situation. If he doesn't have a plan, he could say to us, "I don't have a plan. Do you have a plan?"

What a great way to have prospects ask us for presentations, rejection-free.

- "You know, I feel so unproductive driving all the way to work in the morning, and driving all the way back home at night. What a waste of my time. My next goal is working from home. What about you?"

Maybe we get a quick agreement that our co-worker wants an opportunity to work from home. At the very least, we've planted a seed that may grow inside of our prospect's mind.

- "What do I hate about this job? Cheap coffee and the work takes up all my time. What do I like about this job? Great friends. Do you think maybe we could do something else? Maybe go into business together?"

The "yes" or "no" answer to this question is quick. Why? Because we are not selling a business. We only want to know if our prospect would like to escape the job and be in business with us.

But let's not limit this to opportunity.

Here are some examples of questions to make our prospects think about our products and services.

- "I am tired of exercising, eating funny foods, starving myself ... and having the weight come back. I've decided to lose weight one time, and keep it off forever. What about you?"

And now a positive response makes selling diet products easy.

- "Last year we stayed with my mother-in-law and her 32 cats for our holiday. This year we are taking a real holiday, at a price we can afford. What about you? Feel like taking a real holiday too?"

Our prospect can begin to dream about a holiday that is special. If we sold travel services, we could solve our prospect's holiday problem.

- "I looked at my utility bill last month. You know, our rates won't change unless we do something about it. I made a change to make my bill lower. What about you?"

What can our prospect say? We won't hear many people say, "Oh, I am a victim. I can't do anything about it."

We will hear interested prospects ask us how to change their bill and make it lower.

It is how we start that matters.

There is an old saying: "You can lead a horse to water, but you can't make it drink." Well, that might be true … but we can add a little salt to the horse feed. We can direct the conversation to our prospects' dissatisfaction. Now a conversation about our business can happen more naturally.

Ask negative questions.

Early in our conversations, let the prospects sell themselves.

We can do this with questions such as:

- "Why do you want to invest your time in a part-time business?"

- "Why are you interested in investing more money into your health?"

- "Why do you want to starve yourself just to lose a little weight?"

- "Why would you want to change your current skincare routine?"

- "So, do you think keeping your current plan, working at your job, is going to be the answer?"

These types of questions appear to be negative. However, to answer these questions, our prospects will assume that they want what we have to offer.

What happens? Our prospects sell themselves with their answers. For example:

> **Us:** "Why do you want to invest your time in a part-time business?"

Prospect: "Well, I don't earn enough money in my present job. I can't see myself pushing papers from one side of the desk to the other side of the desk for the rest of my life. I want a change. I thought I could test the waters by trying a part-time business. I don't want to risk what I have, but I do want to try something."

The longer we listen, and the more our prospects talk, the more our prospects will sell themselves.

An interesting fact? Shy people naturally listen more. This gives shy people the advantage when talking to prospects. Why?

When shy people listen, two things happen.

#1. Prospects talk about their problems. Since the purpose of business is to solve prospects' problems, shy people will know exactly what to talk about.

#2. The more prospects talk about their problems, the more prospects sell themselves that they need a solution now. This makes pre-closing easy.

Listening, not talking, is the key to rapport and selling.

Pushback or resistance from prospects?

Some prospects show signs of negativity, impatience or sales resistance. We see this skepticism in their faces, or notice their folded arms.

Here is a little phrase that makes everything better. Simply say, "Here is the short story."

This tells prospects we will be short, to the point, and we won't have any time for disgusting sales techniques. The prospects feel calm, and we can present the short story that sums up our offer in 20 seconds.

Here are some examples.

"So here is the short story. Instead of donuts, you drink our power shake for breakfast. Now you can manage your weight for the rest of your life."

"So here is the short story. The only thing that is different is we will send you a lower bill for your monthly electricity."

"So here is the short story. Use our night cream every night, and you won't have to listen to your skin wrinkle while you lay in bed."

"So here is the short story. Start working with me and get a part-time paycheck. Now you have more money every month."

Is this the only way to reduce pushback or resistance?

No. We should have several ways to disarm negativity from our prospects. Here is another way to relax our prospects and turn off their salesman alarms.

"What would you like to know first?"

Imagine an extremely negative situation. For instance, we are sitting down with our cigar-smoking, used-car-salesman uncle. He coughs and says, "Okay, Sonny. Give me your best sales pitch."

Ouch. We can feel his judgment and resistance. As professionals, we disarm our uncle by saying these words, "So Uncle, what would you like to know first?"

Our uncle thinks, "Hey, you aren't a salesman. You are going to let me talk. Salesmen don't let other people talk. So if I get to talk, let me tell you exactly what I want to know first."

And in that moment, we disable the pushback and resistance from our uncle. He will tell us exactly what question he would like us to answer first. We don't have to guess. We don't have to pull out a presentation book and feel uncomfortable. All we have to do is sit back and listen.

Remember being a victim of one of those long sales presentations? Remember how the salesman talked on and on? And all we wanted to do was ask a simple question. We didn't listen to the salesman. We were busy trying to remember our question and looking for an opening to talk.

Prospects love it when we ask them what they want to know. Prospects hate it when we force on them what we think they need to know.

If we ask them what they would like to know first, then we will never feel embarrassed again. This simple question makes it easy for an open-minded discussion to occur.

So whenever we feel nervous, we can fall back on this easy question. "What would you like to know first?"

Here is what is great about this question. We can use this question at the beginning of our presentation, at the end of our presentation, or even in the conversation before our presentation begins.

No stress. Happy prospects. Saying the right words makes this business easy.

"IF YOU ARE LIKE MOST PEOPLE ..."

Early in our conversations we can use these words: "If you are like most people ..."

Why these words? Because most people want to be like "most people." They will want to agree with whatever we say next.

Want to hear how pleasant this sounds in conversation?

- "If you are like most people, you would love to be your own boss."
- "If you are like most people, you are way too busy to lose weight by going to the gym."
- "If you are like most people, you want to keep wrinkles away an extra 15 years."
- "If you are like most people, your job interferes with your week."

These words make us seem like mind-readers. Prospects will nod and agree with us. This helps open their minds so they can hear the good messages we have for them.

When prospects are on our side and agree with us, everything else is easy.

THE BIG "IF" STATEMENT THAT SELLS OUR PROSPECTS.

There is a way of talking to prospects that helps them decide if they want to fix their problem ... or not.

If they decide they want to fix their problem, we are done. They made a decision before we started. Try it. Here are some examples:

"If going to work, paying the bills, and saving the balance works for you ... great. If not, let's talk."

"If working for your boss, commuting, and getting a few weeks of vacation a year works for you ... great. If not, we should talk."

"If dieting, exercise, and eating funny foods works for you ... great. If not, use our breakfast shake to lose those extra pounds."

"If you can tolerate rip-offs and being taken advantage of ... no problem. If not, use our legal plan."

"If the small wrinkles and lines that come with age are okay with you ... enjoy them. If not, use our rejuvenating night moisturizer."

"If spending the rest of your life working at your job is what you want to do ... okay. If not, let's have coffee."

"If spending the next 15 years making payments on your student loan is something you want to do ... no problem. If not, come with me to a business meeting tonight."

Simple message. Only a few words. And prospects sort themselves out immediately.

THREE GREAT PRE-CLOSING QUESTIONS TO ASK OUR PROSPECTS.

Question #1: "Are you okay with …?"

Help prospects realize the penalty for not taking action. They prefer not to think about the penalty. Instead, they resist change and avoid taking action. This means our prospects will continue to suffer with the pain of their problems.

We ask this question early in our conversation. This gives our prospects plenty of time to decide, "Yes, I need to fix this problem now."

We can tactfully remind our prospects that their "non-action" can make them unhappy with this simple question: "Are you okay with …?"

Here are some examples:

- "Are you okay with taking orders from someone else for 40 years?"
- "Are you okay with someone else telling you how much money you can earn?"
- "Are you okay with only a few weeks' holiday every year?"
- "Are you okay with giving up your freedom to do work that you hate?"

- "Are you okay with working in a job that you have no passion for?"
- "Are you okay with giving up your dreams to work on your boss's dreams?"
- "Are you okay with begging someone else for a raise?"
- "Are you okay with only limited time to travel?"
- "Are you okay with continuing to get by with only one paycheck?"

But what about our products and services?

Here are some examples:

- "Are you okay with starving yourself, and then watching the weight come back when you eat again?"
- "Are you okay with your skin wrinkling a little more every day?"
- "Are you okay with paying the highest electricity rates of anyone on your street?"
- "Are you okay with taking the same old boring vacations, and having to pay for them yourself?"
- "Are you okay with using cheap cosmetics that look … cheap?"
- "Are you okay with putting chemicals inside of your children's mouths twice a day when they brush their teeth?"

Question #2: "What would happen if ...?"

Prospects need to mentally see the benefits of our offer. We can put these benefits in our prospects' minds. But why not make these benefits more powerful? Let's have our prospects create their own version in their minds.

We can get our prospects to sell themselves and see the benefits of our offer with this simple question: "What would happen if ...?"

Here are some examples:

- "What would happen if you didn't have to wake up every morning to go to work?"
- "What would happen if you had more holiday time with the family?"
- "What would happen if you didn't have to spend hours commuting every week?"
- "What would happen if you had an extra paycheck every month?"
- "What would happen if you could retire next year?"
- "What would happen if you had a bigger paycheck for your family?"
- "What would happen if you could take a five-star vacation with the kids?"
- "What would happen if you had more time to work on your own dream?"

But what about our products and services?

Here are some examples:

- "What would happen if you could lose weight one time and keep it off forever?"
- "What would happen if you woke up every morning feeling great, before the alarm clock went off?"
- "What would happen if you could take five-star holidays for the price of a standard hotel room?"
- "What would happen if you could send a personalized greeting card for half the price of a generic store-bought card?"
- "What would happen if your lipstick stayed on your lips all day and you didn't have to worry about touching it up?"
- "What would happen if your skin got younger while you slept?"
- "What would happen if your utility bill was smaller and you had extra money to spend every month?"

Again, this question should be asked early in our conversations. Give our prospects plenty of time to sell themselves.

Question #3: "So what is important about _____ for you?"

Prospects do things for their own reasons, not our reasons. And let's face it, prospects think differently than we do. In most cases, we own a business, they have a job.

We don't know how or why they may be interested in our products or business. We have to find out that information so we can close more effectively. Here is the question that gets information about our prospects' motivations: "So what is important about _____ for you?"

Just fill in the blanks. Here are some examples:

- "So what is important about having a part-time business for you?"
- "So what is important about having an extra paycheck for you?"
- "So what is important about staying home for you?"
- "So what is important about having more free time for you?"
- "So what is important about losing weight for you?"
- "So what is important about saving money for you?"
- "So what is important about being your own boss for you?"

And now we will be talking about what our prospects want to talk about.

Another way to say this is:

- "So why is it important to you to have a part-time business?"
- "So why is it important to you to have an extra paycheck?"
- "So why is it important to you to work out of your home?"

Or we could ask the question this way:

- "So what is the most important reason you want to quit your job?"
- "So what is the most important reason you want to work out of your home?"

But what about our products and services?

Here are two quick examples:

- "So what is the most important reason you want to lose weight?"
- "So what is the most important reason you want to get your natural energy back?"

Decide which question is more natural for you. Then, you can motivate your prospects to move forward now.

REMOVING FEAR FROM OUR PROSPECTS' MINDS.

When we give presentations, what fears do our prospects have?

"I need to find a flaw. If I don't want to do this business, I will need an objection or an excuse to get rid of you."

Now our prospects are looking for reasons not to join. That means that they are not listening to the good things we say.

To fix this problem, we can tell prospects that it is okay for them to tell us that our business is not for them. And, they don't need a reason to turn our business down. We should do this before we start our presentation.

We could tell our prospects this before we start our presentation:

"Let me tell you about my business. And at the end, you can decide if it fits you or not. That is up to you."

Now, the pressure is off our prospects. They can relax and listen to what we have to offer.

What about costs?

Do prospects wonder how much our business will cost? Of course. If they think about the cost throughout our presentation, we won't have their full attention on what we have to offer.

So why not tell prospects how much it costs in advance? Great idea. Here is an example of what we could say:

"Before I show you our business, let me tell you what worries me. When I finish, you will love what you see. But the startup costs might be difficult for you to take out of your budget. Let me ask you, will $499 be a problem for the family budget?"

This opening helps us on many points.

#1: If we wait until the end to tell our prospects about money, what are they thinking the entire presentation? "How much will this cost?" Now, this won't be a problem. Our prospects know.

#2: We tell our prospects that they will love what they are going to see. This puts our prospects in a positive frame of mind. Now our prospects are looking for reasons to join, instead of reasons why not.

#3. If our prospects cannot afford $499, it is better to know this before we start our presentation. If we wait until the end of our presentation to have this discussion, there is too much pressure. If we know there is a money problem early in our conversation, we can talk about options for raising the $499, or adjust our presentation.

#4. Our prospects feel relaxed. We are honest and upfront by telling our prospects the cost in advance. Now, everyone can relax during the presentation.

When is the best time to remove our prospects' fears?

In the beginning, of course.

There is too much pressure on our prospects if we wait until the end of our presentation.

EVERYONE LOVES A STORY.

Especially if the story is all about them. Short stories work better than long stories. Prospects have short attention spans. But we can pre-close prospects before our presentation with a story that they can relate to.

Here is an example of a short story that gets our prospect to participate.

Us: "If your boss offered you a $5,000-per-year raise for learning some new skills, would you do it?"

Prospect: "Of course I would."

Us: "What if your boss then asks you to teach these skills to some of your co-workers in exchange for another $5,000-per-year raise?"

Prospect: "Yes. Sounds good."

Us: "And then if your boss offered another $5,000-per-year raise if you would teach your co-workers to teach those same skills to other co-workers ... how would you feel about that?"

Prospect: "Excellent! That would be awesome!"

Us: "Well, your boss is not making this

offer, but we are. If you join our
business, this is exactly what we
would ask you to do. And, if you took
our business seriously, you could earn
a lot more."

And now our prospect is sitting on the edge of his chair, waiting for our business details. We haven't even started our presentation and our prospect is looking for reasons to join.

When we can relate to prospects by seeing the world through their eyes, they see the advantages of our business or products.

WHY DON'T WE SAY THIS INSTEAD?

A popular soy milk came in a large carton. Near the opening, the directions said:

"Shake well and buy often."

Not quite subliminal ... but I bet these few well-chosen words generated repeat sales.

Do we check the messages we give to our prospects? For instance, we might say:

"Try a bottle of our vitamins and see if you feel better."

But suppose we said:

"It takes 90 days to rebuild our bodies. Take our vitamins for 90 days and see the difference they make."

Hmmm. Now we are selling a three-month commitment instead of a 30-day supply. Little changes in what we say can mean a big difference in our business.

Want another example? Let's say we sold electricity savings. We could say:

"Fill out your request here ... and spend your savings wisely."

When our prospects think about spending their savings wisely, they are making a mental commitment to give us their business.

Another example?

For a business opportunity:

"Fire your boss and sleep in often."

As they imagine sleeping in late, their minds are making a commitment to join our business.

We can help our prospects focus on our benefits by choosing our words wisely.

More questions that help prospects make decisions - now!

We are sitting over coffee with our prospects. No one is relaxed. We know exactly what our prospects are thinking:

- "What if this turns out to be a big mistake?"
- "Are we making the right decision or the wrong decision?"
- "Let's think it over and maybe something will happen so we don't have to commit."
- "What if we try it and it's a disaster?"
- "How long can we put off this decision?"

Tick, tick, tick. Silence. We hope our prospects say something or just make any decision. Everyone wants to move on.

But our prospects keep delaying. They are afraid. They don't realize that "not making a decision" is making a decision to keep things as they are. Yes, a "think it over" decision is really making a "no for now" decision.

We know this. Our prospects don't. Our prospects don't realize that when they delay making a decision about our business, they are making a decision to keep their lives the same.

Keeping their lives the same is okay. But, they should be consciously making that decision instead of having that decision made by default.

I often get the question, "My prospect wants to think it over. How do I get my prospect to make a decision?"

My answer? I say, "Your prospect made a decision already. Your prospect made a decision to stay where he is, to keep his life the same."

Prospects either make a decision to move forward now, or they make a decision to stay where they are.

So here are a few questions that we can ask our prospects. They are innocent, non-aggressive questions. These questions help our prospects make a conscious decision on what is best for their lives.

Here is the best part.

We don't have to ask these questions at the end of our presentation. We can ask these questions before our presentation!

These questions reduce the "I need to think it over" objection. As a bonus, they also pre-close our prospects before we start our presentation.

Here is the first question we can ask.

"What will happen if you don't join our business?"

Of course our prospects will say, "Nothing."

Now we will let the prospects think more about that question for themselves. They will think:

"Well, if we walk away, our lives will be the same. Tomorrow we'll have the same problems we have today. We will wake up to our alarms, fight traffic going to work, come home late after more traffic, grab a quick meal, watch a few minutes of television and … go to sleep. We hate this routine. Something has to change!"

Not a very pretty picture, is it? Now, if the prospects choose to leave everything the same, if they choose to avoid our opportunity … that's okay. They are making a decision. And that is all we ask.

Want a few more questions like this? Let's see if one of the following questions fits our style or situation.

- "If you don't start your own business now, do you see yourself always working for someone else?"

This will get our prospects to think. Maybe they grimace at the idea of asking permission for days off, or not getting the vacation time they want. Or, maybe they want the time freedom to pick up their children from school. Possibly their biological clock makes them an evening person instead of a morning person. Their morning alarm might be the biggest irritation in their lives.

- "What do you think will happen next year if you decide not to make any changes this year?"

This can kickstart their imaginations. They picture their lives like the movie *Groundhog Day*. Every day it is the same routine. Nothing changes. For some people, the boring security of sameness is an anvil holding them down in life.

They desperately want change.

- "Do you think your job routine (five days a week, three weeks of vacation every year) will ever change?"

Our prospects think, "This sounds like receiving a life sentence. Same thing every day … and then we die." Maybe this question will help them dream about a long summer holiday with the family.

- "I see that you are stressing out about risking a change in your daily life. Why not relax and keep your life as it is?"

People like to disagree in conversation. If everyone agreed, conversations would be boring. So now our prospects' tendencies are to disagree with our question. They may try to convince us that they do want change. It is always better when our prospects "sell themselves."

- "You don't have to make a decision to start your own business tonight. Instead, make a decision not to start your own business, and keep your present job routine forever."

Again, the prospects want to disagree with us and say that they want to start their business tonight. We simply pointed out that this is a simple "yes" or "no" decision. Thinking it over was not one of the options.

- "You know, you might be thinking, 'My daily routine isn't so bad. Maybe I will keep living this way.' And that is also a good decision. Do you think that might be best for you?"

Again, the prospects want to disagree with us and say that they don't want to continue with their present routine. By giving them permission to stay where they are, we remain in rapport. The prospects love us, and they might think, "Hey! I would love to work with you!"

- "Would it be okay if you never had to go to work again?"

Wow. Now our prospects are dreaming again. They think, "I haven't dreamed since high school. I got caught up with making a living. What about those dreams I had? If I didn't have to go to work to make a living, I could go back to school and get my music degree. Or, what about backpacking around the world for five months?"

Most people want to do exciting things before they die. But they can't. Why? Because they have to go to work.

Our prospects are thinking, "I hope the opportunity you show me can give me time off from working so that I can chase my dreams."

- "How many more days can you put up with commuting?"

The best time to ask this question is immediately after they complain about the traffic and their commute.

People make decisions to gain things in their lives. But they also make decisions to avoid things in their lives. They may hate commuting so badly that they will do anything to remove commuting from their lives. We could be that solution for them.

- "Life is not forever. What would you really like to do?"

How many people do we know who are trapped in their current circumstances? They feel that they have to keep their jobs to pay the minimum balances on all their debts. They give up hope and wait to die. They forget about those dreams of travel, and time with the family.

But what if someone offered an opportunity to change all that? That someone could be us.

- "How else are you going to get that extra $300 you need every month to get caught up with your bills?"

Now we force our prospect to come up with alternative solutions. Oh wait! They don't have any alternative solutions. Now our prospects realize their best chance for a better life might be with us.

- "How else do you think five pounds a month will go away?"

Yikes! Unless our prospects are delusional, they don't have a plan. Well, they did have plans before, but none of them worked out. That is why they are battling the weight now. They feel they have to commit to our solution.

- "How else do you think you can keep your skin from wrinkling more every evening?"

Our prospects aren't dermatologists. They won't know the latest science or options. Nothing has worked so far. They are still looking for solutions. That is why they are talking to us. They should take our recommendations.

- "How else can you break the pattern of six-day work weeks?"

Prospects get trapped. Big mortgages, car payments, furniture, insurance, lifestyle, eating out, keeping up with their friends … and their paychecks can't support it all. They feel stuck with working more and having less time to enjoy life. Breaking this vicious cycle is hard, but we can offer a way out.

All of these questions remind our prospects that the pain of their problems won't go away by procrastinating on a decision.

So let's make it easy for our prospects.

Remind them to make a conscious decision about their future.

And remember, this technique is rejection-free.

We are not attached to the outcome. We are not responsible for the decisions they make in their lives.

We are only obligated to give our prospects the choices.

The rest is up to them.

It is not the facts. Sometimes it is the story before the facts.

In the early 1970s, I was selling vitamins. Nobody wanted vitamins. Organic? All-natural? Who cared? If you don't want vitamins, it doesn't matter how good the quality is.

The idea of health and nutrition was too new. People believed that health came from an antibiotic.

People didn't care much about their health and well-being, but they did care about being fat. They wanted to lose weight and look good.

My thoughts? "Well, if I couldn't get anyone interested in vitamins, maybe I could reposition my vitamins as diet products."

I still had a problem though. Talking about protein, carbohydrates and fats was boring. Facts are dull. That is why we hate salesmen who dump endless facts on us.

My solution?

Start my own diet club. Not an official diet club, but something more informal. Why? Because I had no budget. No office or gym. I didn't even have a brochure.

So here is how I did it.

To one of my "larger" vitamin customers I said, "Would you like to host a free diet club in your home?" She said, "Yes. Can I invite a few of my friends too? It is a free club, right?" She read my mind.

We agreed to a Tuesday morning diet club. To make the club fun, I explained how it would be more of a social event.

The first meeting had six members - my original vitamin customer and five of her neighbors. I brought my scale and everyone "weighed in" to establish a starting weight. They were hesitant about "weighing in" until I explained that is how we would choose a winner every week.

The fun continued. I did a 30-second lecture on what an exercise would look like if they ever saw one. They smiled as they sat back, chatted, drank coffee, and gorged themselves on cupcakes.

Cupcakes? Yes. Every week the members brought their favorite desserts. It was like a mini dessert buffet at each diet club meeting.

The following week, everyone weighed in. We wanted to see who had lost the most weight from the previous week. The winner lost almost half a pound and received the coveted trophy. Now we had some friendly competition. Everyone wanted to be the winner, so they cheated. One week they wore heavy boots and a thick coat, and the next week they wore the lightest clothes they could find. Everyone had a good laugh at the creative ways they used to win the trophy.

This was a "traveling trophy." I had only one trophy. Last week's trophy winner had to bring the trophy back and award it to the current week's winner.

Had I mentioned vitamins yet? No.

Did I pass out brochures about vitamins? No.

The story continues.

Every meeting I spent one or two minutes explaining some eating tips or an exercise. Then, we would head for the dessert buffet. The friends would stay and chat. Everyone had a great time.

The diet club members appreciated that I organized the club, brought a scale, and bought the traveling trophy. They would ask about my vitamins and purchased them from time to time. Maybe they thought some vitamins would negate the tiramisu cheesecake and chocolate-covered donuts. But each week I delivered vitamins when I came for the diet club.

Did they lose weight? Not much. None in some cases. And yes, quite a few gained weight. But they proudly told their spouses and friends they were members of a weekly diet club. I do know that they were healthier from taking the vitamins they ordered.

And me? I gained quite a few pounds because of these diet club meetings.

I know what you are thinking. "You didn't tell them how wonderful the vitamins were. You didn't tell them about the research, the quality, the amount of vitamin B2, and the natural coating. How could they make a decision to buy when you didn't give a presentation?"

Well, remember the beginning of this book?

People don't make decisions based on facts. And they make decisions before presentations even begin.

Now this makes sense.

It was everything I said BEFORE that made the difference. At the end of the official diet club meeting, the members would just buy vitamins.

What did I say? I used sound bites, word pictures, and descriptive words that created rapport, pre-sold, and pre-closed the members. Want to see some of the words I would sprinkle into the conversation? See if these words spark an interest in health and dieting in your mind.

I wanted to create rapport and trust. So I said, "This salad is rabbit food. Great for rabbits, but not very satisfying for humans."

And the members would think, "Oh wow. He thinks exactly like we do."

I would mention phrases such as:

- "Muffin top."
- "Pinch an inch."
- "Skinny down."
- "Cottage-cheese thighs."
- "Love handles."
- "Orca with legs."

They would think, "Oh my, that is bad. I should be dieting."

I gave them some hope with words such as:

- "Calorie-killers."
- "Willpower in a capsule."

- "The fat assassin."
- "The ultimate fat-blocker."
- "Chocolate-flavored weight loss."
- "Start with a chocolate-flavored dessert shake for breakfast."

I even gave them a vision of success by saying,

- "Fit into your 'skinny jeans.'"
- "Turn your body into a fat-burning machine!"

When I wanted to expand and start more diet clubs, I needed some new distributors to run the clubs. I would add these words into my conversation with the members: "Fatter wallets, thinner thighs." They got the idea that, "Hey! I could earn money and get thin at the same time."

Effective?

Instantly. Word pictures and short, memorable phrases get prospects to take action.

I give this example at my workshops of how one little phrase can make prospects take action:

Imagine I am on a date with a lady. At the end of our romantic dinner, we order a shared dessert. The waiter brings our dessert, piles and piles of chocolate ice cream. Now, ice cream is my favorite food in the world. I love ice cream. I believe that chocolate is one of the four major food groups. My first thoughts? "Sharing is overrated."

But this is a romantic meal. We have to share. But, I want all the ice cream. So how can I sell my date on giving me all the ice cream? How can I get her to make a decision that it is okay if I eat 100% of this ice cream dessert?

Well, there is no time for a sales presentation. Sure I could talk about the benefits of good health, the calorie content of the ice cream, how the saturated fats will cause hardening of the arteries, how the sugar content will lead to diabetes ... but the ice cream will melt during my presentation. I have to act fast. I will have to use a ... sound bite!

As the waiter leaves the table, we look at the beautiful mound of chocolate ice cream. I simply say to my date, "This ice cream will look a lot better on your hips than mine."

Yes, I get all the ice cream.

Done!

You might be thinking, "But if you use that sound bite, you will never get another date with this lady!" True. But let's focus. This is all about who gets the ice cream. We have to have priorities in our lives.

So, no presentation?

No presentation. Everything happened in the conversations during the diet clubs. The small words and phrases pre-closed the members to buy vitamins, get healthy, and attempt to lose weight.

But what about other products?

Let's do more examples of sound bites, word pictures, and descriptive words that pre-close prospects.

Skincare and cosmetics.

What could we say early in our conversations that would get prospects to want skincare and cosmetic products now?

- "I didn't want my face to look older than I am." Ouch! That gets an emotional response immediately. Even though we say these words about ourselves, our prospects imagine that conversation in their heads. This makes it easier to sell "prevention."

- "Well, you know how cheap makeup makes us look … cheap?" What do our prospects think? In their mind, they picture themselves looking less than their best with cheap makeup. Investing in higher-quality makeup just makes sense.

- "I don't want to look like my grandmother, just one wrinkle away from a prune." Well, neither do our prospects. They remember these words because of the humor. And they make an immediate decision to prevent wrinkles. Selling moisturizers is easy.

- "No one wants to leave the house looking like they graduated from the clown school of makeup." Our prospects don't either. Now they want to make sure their makeup is coordinated, not some random selection from a discount store bargain barrel.

More sound bites, please!

Sprinkling a few choice sound bites in our conversation makes prospects decide, "Yes, I want that." And this is all before our presentation.

Here are some skincare and cosmetics examples.

- "Luxurious eyelashes, naturally, without pasting them on."
- "Feels so soft, like a baby's behind."
- "Look like a professional model in just 7 minutes."
- "How to keep our wrinkles away for an extra 20 years."
- "Be the youngest-looking member of the class reunion."
- "A year-round tan without having to bake in the sun."
- "Wrinkle shrinker."
- "Makes us look like the younger sister."
- "Makes our skin younger every night while we sleep."

Can I use the same techniques for health products?

Of course. Let's start by looking at some bad phrases. These should be easy to recognize; they're boring, and kill our chances of a sale.

- "Our multivitamin contains superoxide dismutase to break down potentially harmful oxygen molecules in our cells." (Oh, that is exciting, isn't it?)
- "Our scientist won an award one time and can beat up your scientist." (You are telling me I was stupid and bought something else?)

- "Our ingredients are not only natural, they are supernatural. We put the 'O' in organic." (Too much hype! I smell a sales pitch.)
- "Our pharmaceutical-grade manufacturing processes are ISO-approved." (So what?)
- "Our premium protein shakes have balanced amino acids and are gluten-free and sugar-free. By eliminating excess carbohydrates, we can help manage the body's blood sugar regulation. This will support healthy weight management." (Most people only want to know if the shakes taste good.)
- "Our formulas are unique, patented, registered, and proprietary." (Yawn!)

Yes, these are terrible. The distributors who use these phrases will have to keep their day jobs ... forever.

Enough of these bad phrases. Let's see how the conversations can improve.

Distributor: "I help people over 50 live longer. Would you like to know more?"

Prospect: "Oh yes. Please tell me more."

What decision has our prospect made? It is obvious. Our prospect thinks, "Yes, I want to live longer. You can help me. I want what you have to offer."

And yes, this is all before the sales presentation.

Distributor: "Children are exposed to every known disease and virus when they go to school. I show moms how to protect their children by building up their immune system. Would you like to know more?"

Mom: "Yes. How does that work?"

◇◇◇◇

Distributor: "Growing old … hurts. I help people fix that. Would you like to know more?"

Prospect: "Yes. Tell me now."

◇◇◇◇

Distributor: "There is too much stress these days. Sometimes we marry stress. I have something that can help. Would you like to know more?"

Prospect: "Yes. Tell me more … now!"

Conversations before the presentation are where most prospects make their final decisions. It is not the boring facts that get prospects to decide.

But we want some sound bites that we can use in our conversation too.

Here are some health sound bites that we can use anywhere in our conversations with prospects. Of course, the best place to use these sound bites is early in the conversation, when our prospects are making their final decisions.

- "Instant energy in a capsule."

- "Turns on your energy and makes you a 'super mom.'"

- "Dying early is inconvenient." (Yes, prospects smile, but they do agree.)

- "If we don't take care of our bodies, then where are we going to live?"

- "We can feel like we are 16 years old again, but this time with better judgment."

- "We can save a lot of money on our vitamins by simply dying early." (Okay, a bit cruel, but it does help with the money objection later.)

- "We want more energy than our grandchildren, so they whine, 'Grandpa! Grandpa! Slow down, we can't keep up!'"

- "One of the first symptoms of heart disease is instant death." (A bit dramatic, but it does make prospects think. We are helping our prospects keep their priorities straight.)

- "Wake up every morning feeling like a million dollars."

- "Fall asleep within ten minutes of our heads touching the pillow."

But what about sound bites for my business opportunity?

Okay. We now know that short phrases and sound bites, used early in our presentation, pre-close our prospects.

Let's take this seriously. We want to accumulate an entire library of these sound bites and phrases.

- "Warehouse our babies in daycare." (Yes, this does make moms cringe when they hear this. Maybe they feel guilt. Maybe it strikes home the feeling that they want to be home with their children, but don't have a plan to make that happen.)

- "Wake up at the crack of noon." (Obviously only for people who love staying up into the late hours of the night.)

- "Jobs interfere with our week." (This takes a moment for prospects to process, but then they will remember this forever.)

- "Double our pension in only nine months." (Gets the over-50 crowd excited, because retirement is close enough to seem real.)

- "We don't want to work 45 years like our parents."

- "We call our business the boss-silencer."

- "Turn our minds into wealth magnets."

- "We call our part-time checks 'mortgage-busters.'"

- "Our chance to go from zero to hero!"

- "Leaving the rat race."

- "Take five-day weekends, instead of two."

- "If we hang around four broke people, we can guarantee that we will become number five."

- "The reward for investing $200,000 into a university degree? 45 years of hard labor."

- "Dream-sucking vampire boss, taking little bits of our brain out every day, turning us into human zombies."

Little phrases and sound bites early in our conversation are what prospects use to make decisions.

The secret objection.

Objections are easier to answer when we bring them up before we start our presentation. Here is a common objection that our prospects seldom verbalize.

Yes, they think this objection, but almost never tell us. So why don't we answer this objection for them early? Then they can relax during our presentation.

What is this secret objection?

"But what if I fail?"

Prospects are afraid to take a chance to build their network marketing careers.

There is a lot of uncertainty in our prospects' lives. They have a job now. Is that job secure forever? Of course not. This insecurity gives prospects a lot of stress.

100% of our prospects' income is dependent on their job existing. Prospects aren't stupid. They see the news. Mergers, downsizing, and replacing highly-paid, experienced employees with low-paid trainees is common. This scares our prospects.

To build rapport, we agree with our prospect that these risks exist. Now our networking business looks more like a safety net instead of a risk. Having one more income makes sense.

Another way to illustrate this is to say: "If we lose our job, we may be unable to find another job. But in business, if our business does not work, we can always start another business. Having our own business at least gives us some options."

Having initial failure is okay. It takes time to learn how to build a business. To feel unsure about our success is perfectly normal. The best way to communicate this is with a short story. Here is an example that we can adjust to fit our prospects.

"Imagine we want to learn how to ride a bicycle. We have the desire, but not the skill. Do we know exactly how to ride that bicycle before we start? Certainly not. We start before we know how. But over time, we learn. There will be some temporary failures along the way, but we learn and become successful bicycle-riders."

Next, remind our prospects that the company does not expect them to know how the business works before they start. Of course everything looks difficult at first, because we haven't learned anything yet. We help our prospects feel better by saying that the company has training, plus they have a sponsor - us. And as their sponsor, we can walk with them step-by-step until they learn the skills they need. This gives our prospects confidence. Why? Because we have already learned how to work the business.

To review, let's relax our prospects. Let them know it is normal to feel unsure. They haven't learned anything yet. It is okay to fail temporarily along the way. That is how children learn to walk. And finally, with the company training, and with our help, they can feel secure that over time, they will make their business successful.

If your prospects know all this, they will feel excited about the possibilities of our business, even before we start our presentation.

What is another way to help our prospects overcome their fear of possible failure?

We help our prospect focus on these two facts:

1. Other people have been successful.

2. These people did not have the skills when they started, but they learned.

What is the prospect thinking? Well, if other people became successful, certainly it is possible. These people probably had the same fears. They didn't know how to work this business either.

We can communicate this to our prospect with this little statement:

"I know you can be very successful in this business. I just don't know how fast."

Then, we explain that everyone who starts feels unsure and unequipped. Nobody expects us to know the skills of a brand-new profession before we start. We learn the skills over time. We remind our prospect, "Please don't judge your future success based on what you currently know. You will feel better when you know more after the training."

When the prospects ask, "So how long will it take me to be successful?"

We can answer, "That depends on how fast we learn the new skills, and how fast we meet new people."

MORE MAGIC WORDS TO DISARM NEGATIVE PROSPECTS.

Sometimes we need good words to salvage an uncomfortable situation.

Imagine our worst nightmare. We sit down with our know-it-all pompous neighbor. We want to talk to our neighbor about our business.

Our neighbor leans back in his chair and says, "Okay! Give me your best sales pitch." Ouch. This is an ugly start. A skeptical, negative, unsmiling neighbor.

Where do we start? Do we show him a 20-minute company video? Pull out a PowerPoint presentation? Doing this will only invite sarcasm and criticism from our pompous neighbor.

We need a set of words to neutralize our neighbor's terrible attitude. Our neighbor expects a sales presentation. His resistance meter is overloaded. If we don't have some magic words, we are dead.

No problem for us.

We know how to pre-close. We can turn off the salesman alarm and skepticism of almost anyone with this statement:

"Before I show you how this works, let me tell you what happened to me."

When we say this statement, what happens in our neighbor's mind?

These words tell our neighbor that the sales presentation is not going to happen until ... later. Immediately, our neighbor sets aside his salesman alarm, his skepticism, his too-good-to-be-true filter, and his negative programs.

Guess what our neighbor thinks when we say, "Let me tell you what happened to me."

Inside our neighbor's mind, a little voice says, "Story? You are going to tell me a story? I like stories. Please tell me the story."

Everyone loves stories. We have internal programs that command us to listen to stories.

Think about this situation.

We are at work. We walk by three of our co-workers. One of the co-workers is telling a story. What does our subconscious mind command us to do? Stop and listen to the story. We have a little program in our mind that says, "If anybody, anywhere, at any time, is telling a story, we have to stop and listen to the story all the way to the end. We cannot go on in life until we know how the story ends."

Our negative neighbor is now concentrating on the story, and is not concentrating on making our life miserable.

Stories are irresistible to the human mind. That is why we like Hollywood movies, books, and gossip. Small children, from the moment they can construct a sentence, say, "Mommy, Daddy, please tell me a story."

Our negative neighbor has no defense. His mind focuses on the story. He forgets his negative feelings toward us and our sales presentation.

What can we put in our story?

1. We can tell the story of how we were skeptical, but our experience proved this was a great business.

2. We can tell the story of how we had a great experience with our product.

3. We can tell the story of how our life was before our business, and how life is now.

4. We can tell a story that someone else told us about their success in our business.

What happens inside our neighbor's brain when we tell the stories? His thoughts are swept up into our story. He sees himself in the stories. Our stories could be enough to get a "yes" decision from our neighbor immediately.

Want an example?

Our neighbor says, "Okay. What is this all about?"

We answer, "Before I show you how this works, let me tell you what happened to me."

Our neighbor says, "What happened?"

We answer, "Well, you know John? He never saved anything for retirement. I did not want to be like him. When I saw this part-time business, I got excited. This business could give me a huge part-time income for the rest of my life. I wouldn't have to worry about company pension programs, or government retirement benefits. All I would have to do is get this business started correctly. Then, I could collect money every month for the rest of my life. That is why I was so excited to share this with you. But anyway, let me show you how this business works."

We just delivered our biggest benefits past our neighbor's negative programs, directly into his mind. That was so easy.

And the best part is, we disabled all of his negative defenses.

All this happened, even before we started our presentation.

GET OUR PROSPECTS TO FOCUS ON SOLVING THEIR PROBLEMS.

The purpose of business is to solve people's problems.

But what if people are not thinking about their problems? Then we have to get them to refocus. When their problems are at the front of their minds, they want to solve these problems.

How do we get them to refocus?

Easy. Just start with these words: "Think about your current situation ..."

For example:

> "Think about your current situation. Every month you get a paycheck. After paying the mortgage, the car payments, the credit cards, the taxes, the insurance, the food and more ... how much do you get for giving up a month of your life working for someone else?"

Now what are our prospects thinking? Of course they want to solve that problem. They want a solution now. We don't have to sell them a solution with facts, videos and statistics. All they want is to fix their problem ... and we are there with the solution.

What other openings could we use?

- "Think about your current situation. Every morning the alarm rings …"
- "Think about your current situation. Every time that electric bill comes in the mail …"
- "Think about your current situation. Every morning when you step on the scale …"
- "Think about your current situation. Every time commuting traffic backs up …"

Then, finish the story. Our prospects will see a movie in their minds of this terrible situation.

When prospects want to fix their problems, they will eagerly look for solutions, even before we start our presentation.

MOST PEOPLE LOVE HOW THIS PRE-CLOSES PROSPECTS.

In the book, *"How To Get Instant Trust, Belief, Influence and Rapport! 13 Ways To Create Open Minds By Talking To The Subconscious Mind,"* there is an important phrase. The phrase is "most people." This phrase is very effective for our pre-closing efforts.

When we say "most people," what happens in our prospects' heads? Their automatic programs activate. Their programs say that they want to be part of most people.

Why? Because they want to survive. Early humans learned that if they were a loner, their chances of survival were lower. That is why we will naturally go to a crowded restaurant instead of an empty restaurant. If we discover a brand-new berry, we want someone else to eat the berry first. We don't want to walk through a dark alley late at night by ourselves. We want to walk with a group.

Survival? For us, that means staying with the group, being safe, letting other people go first, and avoiding risks.

When we meet prospects, the programs in their minds are also saying, "Survive! Avoid risk. Be safe. Stay with the group."

When we say the words "most people," their minds run a script that goes something like this:

"Most people. Am I part of most people? Or am I part of fewer people? Not many people are in the fewer people group, so I must be in the most people group. So if I am part of most people, I think like most people. I do things like most people. I am a most people type of person!"

Feel how quickly the decisions happen in our minds when we say things like:

- "Most people like the blue model instead of the red."
- "Most people who get the moisturizer also get the cleanser."
- "Most people feel safer when they have two paychecks a month."
- "Most people want more money."
- "Most people are tired of wasting time commuting to work."

We can feel the instant "yes" decisions in our minds when we hear phrases such as these. So in the beginning of our conversations with our prospects, we can insert a "most people" phrase to help pre-close our prospects.

Want an example?

"Most people I show this business to get excited about it and want to join."

Oh, that was easy. What are our prospects thinking? They think, "I am part of most people. I am sure I will be excited about this business and will want to join." This entire sentence is under the radar, before the presentation. This sentence opens up our prospects' minds so that they will look for reasons to join, instead of reasons not to join.

Pre-closing? It is easy if we say the right words. In some cases, pre-closing opens up our prospects' minds. In other cases, our pre-closing helps prospects make their final decision before we even start our presentation.

Pre-closing works.

Of all the pre-closing techniques in this book, have you found at least one that will work for you? We don't have to use every technique, but we need to use at least one technique.

The more techniques we master, the more options we have when talking to our prospects.

So instead of worrying about high pressure-closing, rejection, and begging prospects for decisions, we will use pre-closing techniques to get immediate decisions in our favor.

Remember, all the techniques in this book work better when we use them.

Choose a technique now. Then, enjoy the results.

THANK YOU.

Thank you for purchasing and reading this book. I hope you found some ideas that will work for you.

Before you go, would it be okay if I asked a small favor? Would you take just one minute and leave a sentence or two reviewing this book online? Your review can help others choose what they will read next. It would be greatly appreciated by many fellow readers.

BIG AL WORKSHOPS

I travel the world 240+ days each year.
Let me know if you want me to stop in your
area and conduct a live Big Al training.

→ **BigAlSeminars.com** ←

FREE Big Al Training Audios
Magic Words for Prospecting
plus Free eBook and the Big Al Report!

→ **BigAlBooks.com/free** ←

MORE BIG AL BOOKS

BIGALBOOKS.COM

Closing for Network Marketing
Getting Prospects Across The Finish Line

Here are 46 years' worth of our best closes. All of these closes are kind and comfortable for prospects, and rejection-free for us.

The One-Minute Presentation
Explain Your Network Marketing Business Like A Pro

Learn to make your business grow with this efficient, focused business presentation technique.

Retail Sales for Network Marketers
How to Get New Customers for Your MLM Business

Learn how to position your retail sales so people are happy to buy. Don't know where to find customers for your products and services? Learn how to market to people who want what you offer.

Getting "Yes" Decisions
What insurance agents and financial advisors can say to clients

In the new world of instant decisions, we need to master the words and phrases to successfully move our potential clients to lifelong clients. Easy … when we can read their minds and service their needs immediately.

3 Easy Habits For Network Marketing
Automate Your MLM Success

Use these habits to create a powerful stream of activity in your network marketing business.

Motivation. Action. Results.
How Network Marketing Leaders Move Their Teams

Learn the motivational values and triggers our team members have, and learn to use them wisely. By balancing internal motivation and external motivation methods, we can be more effective motivators.

The Four Color Personalities for MLM
The Secret Language for Network Marketing

Learn the skill to quickly recognize the four personalities and how to use magic words to translate your message.

Ice Breakers!
How To Get Any Prospect To Beg You For A Presentation

Create unlimited Ice Breakers on-demand. Your distributors will no longer be afraid of prospecting, instead, they will love prospecting.

How To Get Instant Trust, Belief, Influence and Rapport!
13 Ways To Create Open Minds By Talking To The Subconscious Mind

Learn how the pros get instant rapport and cooperation with even the coldest prospects. The #1 skill every new distributor needs.

First Sentences for Network Marketing
How To Quickly Get Prospects On Your Side

Attract more prospects and give more presentations with great first sentences that work.

How to Follow Up With Your Network Marketing Prospects
Turn Not Now Into Right Now!

Use the techniques in this book to move your prospects forward from "Not Now" to "Right Now!"

How To Prospect, Sell And Build Your Network Marketing Business With Stories

If you want to communicate effectively, add your stories to deliver your message.

26 Instant Marketing Ideas To Build Your Network Marketing Business

176 pages of amazing marketing lessons and case studies to get more prospects for your business immediately.

How To Build Network Marketing Leaders
Volume One: Step-By-Step Creation Of MLM Professionals

This book will give you the step-by-step activities to actually create leaders.

How To Build Network Marketing Leaders
Volume Two: Activities And Lessons For MLM Leaders

You will find many ways to change people's viewpoints, to change their beliefs, and to reprogram their actions.

51 Ways and Places to Sponsor New Distributors
Discover Hot Prospects For Your Network Marketing Business

Learn the best places to find motivated people to build your team and your customer base.

Big Al's MLM Sponsoring Magic

How To Build A Network Marketing Team Quickly

This book shows the beginner exactly what to do, exactly what to say, and does it through the eyes of a brand-new distributor.

Public Speaking Magic

Success and Confidence in the First 20 Seconds

By using any of the three major openings in this book, we can confidently start our speeches and presentations without fear.

Worthless Sponsor Jokes

Network Marketing Humor

Here is a collection of worthless sponsor jokes from 25 years of the "Big Al Report." Network marketing can be enjoyable, and we can have fun making jokes along the way.

Start SuperNetworking!

5 Simple Steps to Creating Your Own Personal Networking Group

Start your own personal networking group and have new, pre-sold customers and prospects come to you.

How To Get Kids To Say Yes!

Using the Secret Four Color Languages to Get Kids to Listen

Turn discipline and frustration into instant cooperation. Kids love to say "yes" when they hear their own color-coded language.

BigAlBooks.com

ABOUT THE AUTHORS

Keith Schreiter has 20+ years of experience in network marketing and MLM. He shows network marketers how to use simple systems to build a stable and growing business.

So, do you need more prospects? Do you need your prospects to commit instead of stalling? Want to know how to engage and keep your group active? If these are the types of skills you would like to master, you will enjoy his "how-to" style.

Keith speaks and trains in the U.S., Canada, and Europe.

Tom "Big Al" Schreiter has 40+ years of experience in network marketing and MLM. As the author of the original "Big Al" training books in the late '70s, he has continued to speak in over 80 countries on using the exact words and phrases to get prospects to open up their minds and say "YES."

His passion is marketing ideas, marketing campaigns, and how to speak to the subconscious mind in simplified, practical ways. He is always looking for case studies of incredible marketing campaigns that give usable lessons.

As the author of numerous audio trainings, Tom is a favorite speaker at company conventions and regional events.

CPSIA information can be obtained
at www.ICGtesting.com
Printed in the USA
BVHW061343010719
552379BV00020B/1352/P

9 781948 197007